1. A Lover's Tale

Absconded from many a-care,
Was bemoaned, yet away;
Like a rustle, my heart was struck,
My soul was reeled open.
Yet unsure of the glimpse,
Resistance was not an option;
Though I tried but to no avail,
Like a flood, it swept open my heart.

Like a smile on a new born,
Promising as it was, yet untrue;
Now, my heart surrendered with no retreat,
Just to realize what a shadow it was.

Oh! Like the pain of a woman in labor,
But the future was a mirage;
Coming I'd no help to render,
Still became a necessary end.

Now I have learnt, though a bitter pill,
Yet I wish not to let go;
As a deep cut in my heart it is,

But my love I cannot undo.

2. A TRIBUTE TO TANZANIAN PRESIDENT:

Magufuli Bows!

An Icon, A trailblazer,
Elected by Tanzanians,
For Tanzanians.

He passed,
And a path was created,
Lived,

And a new Tanzania was birthed.

The Airspace was adorned by Air
Tanzania,
Magufuli rewrote their story.

Selfless and transparent,
One of Africa's finest,
A rare species,
Of Tanzania's descent.

Irreplaceable John,
Being lowered down,
Into the grave,
A home for most braves.

Had to bid farewell,
But we know it's well,
Your imprints is forever,
As you into eternity rover.

3. Are you my Angel?

I'm the guy in the hood
Being swayed into diverse mood
All in a bid
To find a bride.

I'm the guy in the hood
Always in boyhood
Jumping up and down
Not ready to settle down.

I'm the guy in the hood,
Preying on the feminine-hood
With no hope of being changed
Cos I've been estranged.

I'm the guy in the hood
Known in the neighborhood
Always playing Hollywood
Right from my childhood.

I'm the guy in the hood
In need of an angel
Not necessarily from Los Angeles
Cos I seem to be changeless.

Are you my angel?
To save this wandering soul
Cos every guy can change
Once he finds his angel.

4. Ask Yourself:

1. It takes a task
   to ask,
   To unmask
   The man beneath.

2. Living a Lie,
   Cruising in Crime;

A man is doomed
By such a mask.

3. The truest truth,
   Of a man's life-state
    Is a function
     Of Self-ask.

4. Have you
   Asked Yourself:
   So, you won't
   Be asked out of eternal bliss.

5. Attaining Value!

Life is not a bed of roses,
Five times to school we go,
Enduring the teachers' lashes,
Just to attain something in Life.

Life is full of ups and downs,
Only the willing survive,
And the Determined possess the land,
But the Feeble-minded,
Egress into extinction.

Amidst the perils of life,
Lies the pleasure thereof,
Treading with patience through its billows,
Thrusts you into the limelight of success.

Tracing through a high temperature,
The worth of gold unfolds,
As the exposure of cassava flour to a hot pan,

Begat the Value craved,
So, sweating through life's hurdles,
Leaves the imprints of success.

Jostling to unmask the true face of life,
Likened to taking a walk through a
mountainous environ,
A steady slide through its atlas,
Eases off life's plight,
Marshalling Life's beauty.

The wild flower grows in the desert,
The toughest part of the planet,
As she awaits the rain,
With bravery, she reaches to the sun,
Making her to bloom.
Courage defined, worth emulating.

6. Bring Back those Days!

Bring back those days
I was young and innocent.
With no fear as a saint.

Bring back those days,
I was pure and full of bliss,
With no fear of loss.

Bring back those days,
I was a child,
With no fear to slide.

Bring back those days,
I was not toiling,
But always smiling.

Bring back those days,
I will sit and cry,
Because I was still young to try.

Bring back those days,
My heart was at peace,
With no fear of being teased.

Bring back those days,
I was sound and bold,
With no fear of being sold.

Bring back those days,

When everything seem perfect,
With no defect.

7. Don't Say I'm Just a Child!

Don't say I'm just a child!
Where you were created for a tide.
And made for a purpose,
Which you must fulfill,
Lest you be disposed.

Don't say, I'm just a child!
Right from the womb,
You were carved,
Wearing a crown,
To save a generation from being starved.

Don't say I'm just a child!
For you have been anointed,
Unto a time appointed.
Though the world be hostile,

Be not afraid to try.

Don't say, I'm just a child.
For those you covet,
Were once in the shoe,
You now neglect,
And refuse to pursue.

Don't say I'm just a child!
For in you is a river,
To water a many,
For them to thrive,
Though you don't yet have a penny.

Don't say I'm just a child!
For your Maker above,
Is looking unto you below?
Even though you don't have a cue,
But that's true.

8. Give A Care!

Everybody is born to care,
It's something we were meant to share.
Not to keep to ourselves all alone.

If we make a room for someone new,
It doesn't mean there's less for you.
It does means that our circle has grown.

Love knows,
Love grows,
Bigger than before,
In your heart.

There's always more,
Its magic,
The more you give it away,
The more love comes back to you,
Everyday.

9.Golden Mum!

Young and Athletic,
Blessed with nature's gift of intellect,
Her marital journey began.

Innocent and Brilliant,
The story of a young teenage girl,
Unfolded.

Looked as if it was fate,
but became an art wroth by
An invisible divine hand.

This young flower,
that looked so fragile,
has come forth with lovely branches in her
likeness.

Redeeming a dynasty,
Afamefula came forth.
in the midst of friendly foes,
Chizobem accompanied.

After four long years of not being heard,
A voice named Onu, emerged who will later
be christened Daniel, for the task ahead.

When the world around saw defeat,
The Divine invisible hand granted her victory,
who was called Victor.

Men saw hopelessness,
But Akajiuwa gave her Hope, and assured her
to Hope-well!

Then, as a seal to the promise made,
Her heart was gladdened,
When Gladys arrived.

She's turned Golden,
after a three decades plus marital journey.
though it hasn't been funny.

She is Hope, Faith, Patience, Grace, Mercy,
Love, Sacrifice, Dedication, Diligence, Virtue
Wisdom personified.
Happy Fiftieth Birthday Mum.

I love 💕 you to the moon.

10.   Lost in The Service!

Just like a bee,
I became busy,
That my Maker I may please,
Looking for a moment to cease.

The table I prepared,
Which was suggested,
By The Lord's visiting,
Not knowing I'm missing it.

I chose the good,

So not to be rude,
But there was a better,
Which was what matters.

Though I am Martha,
But I was stuck with merry,
While the Mary,
Settled for what mattered.

I served,
But I starved.
She settled,
But was satisfied.

I cared to serve,
Then I was carried away.
The other on His feet sat,
And it paved a way.

I cried out,
Cared not that I alone suffer in servitude,
Not knowing what a pearl I'd lost,
Except for mercy, I almost was lost serving.

11.　　Love Happened!

Made in His image,
Which attracted the devil's rage;
Eden's home was lost,
Which was too much a cost.

Just a bite;
Costs the right.
Losing the glory,
Thus, began the story.

Behold, I hid,
But He took the lead
To search for me,
For no price of mint.

He took Calvary's walk,
Too painful to talk,
In amazement, I thus asked,
What happened?
He answered thus-Love happened!

12.   Memory Lane of the Nigerian State:

Dividing the spoils Africa
(In the Berlin conference),
The western region became British share,
Being situated in the region,
Nigcria fell under the British colony.

Under the watch of Lord Lugard,
Followed the 1914 Amalgamation of the
south and the north.

Becoming the most populous black race,
Flora Shaw gave her its nomenclature.

In a bid to ease of the British burdens, Zik and
Belewa pitched against the British masters.
After long years of bearing the British yoke,
1st October 1960, gave birth to the dawn of
freedom to Africa's most populous race.
Following the back-off of the British Lords,
The mantle fell on the Great Zik,
Taking the new born nation further,
She became a republic in 1963.

Blessed by nature's fertile soil, Agriculture
became was the source of her livelihood.
After long years of tilling the soil,
The southern region gave birth to her
treasured spoil, 'oil' in 1958.

Jostling for power control,
Her lands turned a war-front.
Through the menace of military coups,
Her elites and nobles fell back to mother-
earth.

Leading the coup frontiers,
Kaduna Nzeogu, Ironsi, Abiola, Abacha and
the likes became victims.
After long years of power gamble,
By the military,
Obasanjo wore a civilian skin into the
country's leadership in 1999.
Becoming slaves in a free land,
Ojukwu clamored for freedom
For his Igbo brothers;
Gowon opposing Ojukwu's freedom
agitations,
A 30-month (from 1967-1970) war ensued
between the Igbo brotherhood and the rest.

After such an audacious freedom attempt,
One Nigeria prevailed;
Amidst her ethnic controversies,
Her diversity remains her backbone.

13.   Mother Earth!

Oh! Mother Earth!
Void and formless,

In the midst of utter darkness,
You were enclaved on the surface of the deep.
Hovering over the surface of the deep,
The Creators Spirit drew your architectural
design.

Oh! Mother Earth!
Within six-long days of labor,
By the creator's word,
The beauty of what is seen today,
Came into limelight,
Ushering in the Master's plan for thee.

Oh! Mother Earth!
Born amidst seven brother planets,
With only a sister-planet, Mars,
You glow with beautiful moon at night,
And the fierce sun brightens your day.

Oh! Mother Earth!
You defend your territories by your
Lithosphere,
With great mineral deposit enclosed thereof.
Sheltering your heirs with your Atmosphere,

Administering the breath of life in the midst
of it.

Oh! Mother Earth!
You Hydrosphere,
Quenches thirst and irrigates lands,
The aquatic lives find a home in it.

Oh! Mother Earth!
Beneath your belly lies precious stones,
Your surface is adorned with beautiful forest
of trees;
Providing shelter for your wild lives.
Far above in your airspace,
The birds take their dwelling.

Oh! Mother Earth!
You are the Creator's gift to mankind!
Beloved and Cherished among thy brethren.
We uphold thee, Mother Earth!

14.   My Story at a Glance: Twenty-Seven

It was on the wee hours
Of that faithful Eke day
When the birds
Were in their nest still
When the trees
Dance at no sound of music
When the young day
Was still clothed with blackness
When the minds of men
Were still on rest mode
Everything was beautiful and calm
The angels were on assignment,
Setting the stage
For the arrival of him
That is to be brought forth
The mother travailed,
Just for him to prevail
So he can avail the world
The journey began
As that tiny
But innocent voice

Came forth
Announcing the beginning of an era
Then he turned one
Two came, three passed
Four, and behold five
He was taken to the playground
Of the mighty
Where each man
His destiny got shaped
Six, seven, eight, nine and ten

A new chapter began
Eleven, leaving childhood
Twelve, thirteen
A point where everything seems interesting,
and attracting
Fourteen, fifteen, sixteen
Came to a turning point
Met with his creator
Which changed his view
Seventeen and eighteen
The end of an era

Moving on
To explore beyond his shore
Nineteen, twenty
Filled with innocence
The end of two decades of living
Twenty-one, two, three
Completed diploma
The crave for success
Four, and twenty-five
Silver-jubilee
Became a lion
Twenty-six
Broken innocence
Things falling apart
Yet with a will to succeed
Added a one
And today, Twenty-Seven,
Twenty-Eight, experience grows,
The journey continues!

15.   Silver-spoon

Growing up has been a journey,
Birth into a world of penury,
Surrounded by lots of needs unmet,
Filled with desires yet to be satisfied,
Luxury seems to be a dream impossible.

I have heard men talk about silver-spoon,
I wondered why I wasn't opportune with a
spoon,
I grew up eating with bare hands,
Longing for a spoon, yet to have,
Wish I don't wait in vain.

Yeah, though a spoon I'm yet to have,
But while the time is yet to come,
I, with my hands gat to feed,
Till come a day, when I'd get a spoon,
Not just a spoon, but a sliver-spoon.

As crazy as it sounds, but not a wish,
It's a goal, my life is bent on,
Till it comes to pass,
Like a flint, I set my face,
Never to relent nor give up!

16.   Tale of Dynasty!

What seemed like a journey,
Turned into an adventure;
Leading to untold discoveries,
Hidden truths unveiled.

The story begins…

Caught in awe of nature,
Wandering into the beauties beyond,
In a land too far to be near,
With the welcoming sounds birds chirping.

Surrounded by ruckus and rumblings,
Traversing into the jungle search,
Seeking a maiden for the land,
Comes a wrangling tale.

Pursuing the course of the custom,
In a bid to maintain dynasty,
A past walked away from,
Comes playing back.

Alas, the maiden,
Turns out to be a product of the past,
Shooting out from life lived in the past:
Truth uncovered at last!

17.   Tell Mr. President!

Tell Mr. President,
He'd turned our hope
To a rope.

Tell Me President,
His words was supposed to be his bond,
But it has turned on us a bondage.

Tell Mr. President,
His promise of Change
Has turned on us a Charge.

Tell Mr. President,
Those hailing voices of Sai Baba in 2015,
Has turned to wailing voices in 2021.

Tell Mr. President,
That Our Unity in Diversity,
Has, under his watch turned to Diversity in
Unity.

Tell Mr. President,
That lives in war-torn Afghanistan are more
secured,
Than lives in His Nigeria.

Tell Mr. President,
Upon His campaign against GEJ when
Chibok girls were kidnapped,

Dapchi girls went missing under His watch.

Tell Mr. President,
The Future of the Unborn
Are under the mercy of the Chinese in their
land of birth, courtesy of His Chinese debt.

Tell Mr. President,
That before he came with his juicy promises,
Petrol was #87,

Dollar was less that #200,
Life was Cheaper...
Was this the Change he promised?

Tell Mr. President,
That Niger
Is, 'ia' short of Nigeria.

Tell Mr. President,
That he is presiding over Nigeria,
And the impact is reaped by Nigerois.

Tell Mr. President,
The Citizenry,
Are running out of Patience,
That it is now or never.

18.   The Dreamer!

A Dreamer
A Visioner
So I was framed

Scary is the Dream
Makes many to scream
But it can't be trimmed.

They saw it as impossibility
But I know I was in for possibility
Cos the future belongs to Dreamers.

Be A Dreamer today.

19.   The History of Uburu-Adu at a glance:

The Maiden Called Uburu.

In the wake of a new millennium,

And the unfolding of times,

Comes a pretty maiden,

In the guise of a He,

Into the virgin land,

Situated in the rising of the sun,

Surrounded by precious waters,

Which made the land the jealous of many,

Originally called Mburu, but now called
Uburu, a white-mistake.

This maiden,

In a bid to respond to nature,

Settled in this virgin land,

Whose waters remains a treasure,

Gave rise to fourteen brave damsels,

Coming in masculine guise,

Endowed with natures gift of intellect,

Became the envy of many.

Being surrounded by body of waters,

Got linked to people from the outside world,

Her invaders in the guise of admirers,

Wearing a white flesh,

Enticed her nobles with a sweet poison,

Wearing a name 'civilization',

Took away the fruits of her wombs,

In exchange to baits,
Meant to devour her.

Some greedy fellows,

In a bid to rise above others,

Betrayed their motherland,

Embracing these friendly enemies,

Sold out the heirs of Adunshiegbe,

Who their placenta lie still,

In their ancestral home.

Into the hand of the white witches,

Becoming donkeys to them,

Losing their freedom.

These invaders, in the guise of admirers,

Abusing the maiden's nomenclature,

Called her 'Uburu',

Defiled her belief in her 'Chi',

Known as 'Ngeneukwenu',

Who she believed has been the reason for her
        strength,

Introduced her to a new worship,

Chukwu Okike Abiama, who can only be
        accessed through His son,

Embracing the new worship,

She was pierced,

Her unity got wounded.

The white witches,

To appease the land,

Defiled her use of herbs from her forest,

Built a hospital for her sick in 1912,

Weakening her farming power,

Established a school for her heirs in 1913,

In her ignorance,

The stubborn heirs were educated,

By the white witches.

Giving them the taste of the new life.

# 20.	The Human Condition in a Cultural Society:

Hustling Up North.

Went away from a land so green and fertile,

To seek greener pastures in a desert soil.

Ready to bear our toil,

Yet, you're bent on making it futile.

Believing the One Nigeria Slogan,

Not knowing that it is all but a Trojan.

In the midst of their huts and caves,

We sited mansions to meet our craves.

Under their scorching sun,

Yet as if it's all fun.

Ignoring our crying sons,

So we can meet up the demands of their form.

We had high hopes,

But it on us turned ropes.

Thanks to you, not giving us a cue,

That the North,

Is filled with wrath,

Against us from the East,

Because of our ease,

Of adapting to your clime,

Which is no crime.

We came with our life,

But you went into strife,

In a bid to strangle our efforts,

Yet, we gave you our supports,

Changing the narratives of your environs,

Uncovering your errors.

You detected our attire,

Yet of you we were not tired.

Our menu were compromised,

But with you we continued.

Your drums was of war, and made our lives
hell,

But we gave thee peace and thy shores
upheld.

All was against our worth,

Yet we strive for the prize.

21.   The Woman I love!

She is elegant
Making my heart to pant
Spotless like a dove
With her I want to rove.

I summoned courage
And brought her to stage.
For in my heart's page
Has, she taken me hostage.

A perfect picture
For my future
Looking at her curvature
I almost lost my posture

She captured my heart
With her beautiful art
Gorgeous soul
In the feminine fold.

I love you Special!